Here's the Tea

Here's the Tea
A Poem and Rhymes Book

Teresia Simmons-Ursch

Tampa, Florida

This book is a work of fiction. The names, characters and events in this book are the products of the author's imagination or are used fictitiously. Any similarity to real persons living or dead is coincidental and not intended by the author.

The views and opinions expressed in this book are solely those of the author and do not reflect the views or opinions of Gatekeeper Press. Gatekeeper Press is not to be held responsible for and expressly disclaims responsibility of the content herein.

Here's the Tea: A Poem and Rhymes Book

Published by Gatekeeper Press
7853 Gunn Hwy, Suite 209
Tampa, FL 33626
www.GatekeeperPress.com

Copyright © 2023 by Teresia Simmons-Ursch
All rights reserved. Neither this book, nor any parts within it may be sold or reproduced in any form or by any electronic or mechanical means, including information storage and retrieval systems, without permission in writing from the author. The only exception is by a reviewer, who may quote short excerpts in a review.

Library of Congress Control Number: 2022948581

ISBN (paperback): 9781662934148

eISBN: 9781662934155

v

*I would like to dedicate this book to my daughters
Alexus and Alysha.
You were my inspiration for writing this book.
I was going through a very difficult time in my life
when I wrote this book.
Your love and commitment to me made me push through.
Your support was amazing during my trial.
Thank you and my deepest love to you both
for your ongoing support.*

Contents

I Can	1
Daughters	2
Abuse	3
Like Crabs in a Bucket	4
Creeping	5
Connection	6
Rock Bottom	7
Porch Gossip	8
Intuition	9
Growing Up	10
Growing-Old Humor	11
I Ain't No Barbie	12
Suicide	14
Lies	15
Friendship	16
I Am a Mother	17
Silent Screams	18
Incarceration	19
Locked Up	20
A Simple Crush	21
Just One Night	22
Drink of the Flesh	23
Sweet Passion	24
Black Coffee on the Sultry Side	25
Broken Trust	26
Love Emotions	27
Take Me Away	28
Marriage Proposal	29
Love	30
Romance After Dark	31
You Were the One	32
Soul Mating	33
Tis So Sweet	34
Chocolate Child	35
Time Dissipates	36
You Bring Me Peace	37
No Longer at Liberty	38
Storm in Spring	39
A Child's Room	40
View from a Park Bench	41
Visualized Portrait	42
Reflections of a Man	44
Satan's Introduction	45
Lord, Lord	47
A Time to Heal	48
Prayer	49
Heavenly Art	50
Am I Condemned	51
Part-Time Christian	52
Garden Rescue	53
Weed Picker	55
At Rest	57
God's Promise	58
Love Fizzes	59
Love	60
Unsound Mind	61
Little Bennie	62
The Fat Rat	63

I Can

Colored man with a plan
Though they say I can't
"Can't" gave me the will to do what I want.
Someday I'm gonna run this country
Do what no man thought he could do.
Because they said, "You can't,"
So you won't and don't.
Caution and proceed with a plan
Attempt to make it happen.
Navigate your plan to existence
Triumph, you stuck at it when everyone else quit.
"Can't" made me a winner
Cause you said I couldn't
When I knew the possibilities.
In my mind I saw time.
"Can't" stood in the debts of nothing
Using time to do something.
Something I had planned
When you said "can't," knowing I can.

Daughters

Raise your daughters to be free
Build them up as strong leaders.
Show them how to follow, knowing how to lead.
Train their eyes to see the world as a whole
Share experiences of stories untold.
Tell them it's okay to be spontaneous
Stepping out, risking as things are changing.
Let them know they can move mountains
Thinking believing their opportunities are countless.
Appreciate their thoughts, using their ideas
Explain that dreams can become real.
Raise your girls to become personal with Christ
Assuring that God is the balance to life.
Love your daughters so they too will love
Feeling beautiful inside, confidence that shows.
Ameliorate your girls, protect your daughters
As adults they'll strive and work their hardest.

Abuse

I gave you my heart
Watching you tear it apart.
My dignity stripped
As if beaten with a whip.
You say you're sorry
Promised a better tomorrow.
When you got angry
You fussed with file language.
When you slapped my face
I only think of hate.
Your hands choking my neck
Until I'm out of breath.
Eyes looking at me cold
As you rip my clothes.
Oh, how I tried to escape
The abuse and the rape.
Putting a gun to my head
You threaten to kill me dead.
Just to prove your point
You kicked me once.
When you blacked my eye
I covered for you and lied.
Forbidden a car, no job, no friends
Our house is where you kept your secrets in.

Like Crabs in a Bucket

Look at me, I made it first
But like a crab in a bucket
Snap, pull, then jerk.
Back at the bottom, boiling hot
Watching you crawl about to reach the top.
I'm crawling, snapping, tryna move back up
Stepping on those working harder than us.
Even though you're at the top
You ain't going nowhere
Like a crab in a bucket
Snap, pull, then jerk.
Crawling at the bottom is where we'll be
Because pulling each other down
Is what we're used to seeing.
Stabbing each other in the back
Is the reason we're down matter of fact.
You won't get no where, doing others dirty
There's a thing called karma, so be worried.
Crawling back up, making my way
Snap, pull, then jerk, the bottom I lay.
You're crawling, snapping, not looking back
Snap, pull, then jerk, now at the bottom of the stack.

Creeping

Creeping, sneaking, can't get caught
Running, dodging, unable to walk
Hiding, peeking, afraid to be seen
Secret, hidden, kept quiet from friends
Whispering, hushing, did they hear
Jumping, flinching, full of fear
Hurtle, scuttle, don't recognize me
Queasy head pains, losing sleep
Can't share it, don't do it
In the end you won't lose it.

Connection

Never can I disown you
Sharing bloodlines through your veins
Something I cannot change.
Even though you show me disrespect
The day you were born, never regret.
Brisk with the tongue forbearing nothing.
Though sometimes I cross your mind
You leave me sanguine, other times revolted.
These are my repercussions, loving mother.
Door open, my arms spread wide
Not proud of my ornate pride.
Unconditional love seals our unity
Secateur could not cut the tie.
Disowning you is not possible
Death unable to defeat the unstoppable.
You and I are bound eternally
Disowning you, doing so is impossible.

Rock Bottom

Spring up, you spinster, you've hit rock bottom.
Only one way to go, that's up!
Ain't nothing down there but despair
Get moving, woman, fix yo hair.
Laying curled, mad at the world
Thinking so low, nowhere to go.
Only one way to go, that's up!
You got to eat, get on your feet
The rent is due, whatcha gon' do.
Sit and whine, waste more time.
G'on, woman, take a bath
Afterwards we chat and laugh.
My friend, lets loose the mood
Stop rolling them eyes, change ya groove.
Only one way to go, that's up!
Out that tub, off your butt
You can't stay stuck in a rut.
Rock bottom can only open doors
Girl, if you don't get off that floor.
Sprawled out, don't make me shout.
Only one way to go, that's up!
Put on them clothes before I fuss.
That's right, girl, get it together
To get to the top you can't lie there forever.
Only one way to go, that's up!
Don't take long, we gon' miss the bus.

Porch Gossip

OOH yeah, she's a nasty neighbor
She'll turn up her nose, don't do no favors.
Uum hum, thinks she's uppity-up
Somebody ought to pull that stick from her butt.
Oh, girl, she thinks she runs this block
Told her myself, minus this chicken from the flock.
Did you notice how she waved at you
Swung her hand at you as if "fly shoo."
Well, she does keep a pretty nice yard
She spends a lot of money trying to impress us with her cars.
Everyone says she's bitter as a witch
Keep them eyes open, don't miss a trick.
That women sho' points her finger at us
When it's her house that's in a ruckus.
Always acting like she so bad
You can tell she's unhappy, that's sad.
That woman always starts a fight
Can't you see the facade, she ain't bright.
No one visits, we know why
It's that selfish behavior, that's why.
One day she'll grow old and alone
There will be no one to help her
When she's dying alone at home.

Intuition

I knew it before I saw it
I saw it before I recognized it.
I had the answer before the question
I question already having the answer.
I felt it before it happens
It happens, not sure why.
Why it happens brought light
Light shines on the reason.
I reason for the purpose
The purpose I know, but why
I feel what I feel
I feel what is there.
Why do I know by what I feel
The instincts of tuition, how strong.
Intuition gives insight into the unknown.
Oh, how blessed to have intuition.
I have intuition, but God sees it all
God knows all, and that doesn't take intuition.

Growing Up

Project kid, five in a room
Daddy had to spray for roaches.
Struggling hard to keep us stable
Always a hot meal on the table.
School right across the street
Lucky to have a new pair of shoes on our feet.
Cause Ya Po, nobody has to know.
Mom dressed us in nice clothes,
"Get to school," learn them books
My five kids won't be no cook.
No boys, leave them alone
Grab them books, hurry home.
Think Imma let you waste your life
Dem dir boys ain't worth the price.
Shallow men go for looks
Smart men want looks, good in books.
Study your lesson so you can decide
The time you want to become a bride.
Stop moving around, pay attention
Cause there's something I forgot to mention.
You smart, gon' be something
Imma make sure of that, pumpkin.
These here projects are your steppingstone
One day baby, you gon' own a home.
Give mamma some sugar and one of them hugs
After you take this slipper and whack that "bug."

Growing-Old Humor

Looking in the mirror as the years roll by
I noticed the crow's feet underneath my eyes.
My hair once thick now very thin
From the kitchen home perms that split my ends.
Nice firm breasts I've always had
If you saw them now you would say they sag.
Had a body like one of them magazine models
Now when I walk everything bounces and wobbles.
I used to be able to walk to my chair
Now I have a walker to support me there.
Nice-fitting panties to fit my rear end
No control of my bowels, now I wear Depends.
Teeth once strong to chew my meat
Now on my sink you'll find false teeth.
Had a memory sharp and good at first
Now I keep forgetting where I put my purse.
Remember that Mustang I drove like lightning?
Now I catch the bus, they revoked my license.
Aging is something you can't avoid
Just be careful
Not to slip on the floor.

I Ain't No Barbie

Do you think I am your Barbie doll?
I've wondered time again, haven't spoken it loudly.
Wore my hair curly, clipped out of my face
You told me to perm it and wear it straight.
My skin was natural as I wore my hair
You insisted that I get a makeover with Fashion Fair.
I like my clothes to be nice and modest
When I looked in my closet only Apple Bottoms.
Picked studded earrings to match my suit
Opened my jewelry box, they were replaced with hoops.
Feet liking Naturalizers because the way they feel
You gave them to the Goodwill, replacing them with heels.
Occasionally I slouch just a little bit
Etiquette classes you scheduled to teach me how to sit.
Spoke a little slang until the other night
You said, "Stop speaking ghetto and speak like the whites."
Had a compact mirror that my momma bought
Looking in it I frowned with the wildest thought,
Yes, he thinks I'm his barbie doll
Changing me, flaunting me, acting proud.
It's over, I'm done, I'm changing back
I even lost weight because he said I was fat.

Here's the Tea

I'm gonna tell this man I ain't no Barbie
And if he tries it again, he'll be sorry.
I kick him to the curb like kicking rocks
Throw his stuff out on the sidewalk in a cardboard box.
He'd better take heed of the things I've said
If he wants to sleep in my poster bed.

Suicide

I was determined to commit suicide
Like an idiot I thought I wanted to die.
My first choice was to take some pills
It was easy and didn't take no skills.
I didn't drink water like the rest of the folk
Instead, I grabbed the pills and a bottle of coke.
Sitting on the bed swallowing them down
Then I lay there without making a sound.
After twenty minutes I felt a little weak
I knew it was time for my final sleep.
I told God to take me now
He had other plans, I had found.
Thinking it's the end and looking at the ceiling
In the pit of my stomach, I got a sick feeling.
In a matter of seconds, I began to burp
Then the scariest thing happened, my body began to jerk.
The silly thing was I forgot to eat
I realized it when I threw up all over the sheets.
As I barfed up all of those pills
My life flashed before me and gave me the chills.
Boy, was I lucky God stood by my side
Putting a kink in my plans called suicide.

Lies

Lies are like a fungus that you scratch and spread
Spreading like lice in an unwashed head.
Lies are like fleas, they travel everywhere.
Lies resemble garbage that hasn't been dumped
When you open your mouth, it smells like funk.
Lies are said to be untruths
The one who spreads them should lose their tooth.
Lies draw attention like a wounded bat
Bruises, scars, too deep to correct.
Lies are like germs that catch you off guard
They can sicken you like an infection that spreads to the heart.
Lies are like hate that causes confusion
Like a head bump that ignites a contusion.
The tongue spreads lies until it's satisfied.
Stabbing, cutting to its center core
As a knife cutting a roast at a smorgasbord.
Lies resemble a cracked crystal vase
It appears ugly when you look at it's face.
Lies can get you killed just as fast as they spread.
The lie will come back and haunt you one day
No one will believe another word you say.
A man who tells lies will bury himself
They'll lay as an old rug underneath a bookshelf.

Friendship

A friend catches your tears and chases your fears.
A friend holds your hand when you want to make a stand.
A friend stands by you through the very tough roads.
A friend creates sweet memories that you'll always hold.
A friend will never criticize, but correct you when you're wrong.
A friend will encourage you to continue to grow strong.
A friend is like a sunflower blowing with the wind, able to bend.
A friend is a very attentive listener.
A friend listens to your problems and tries to solve them.
A friend keeps private your innermost secrets.
A friend speaks out and has your back.
A friend never cowers when the enemy attacks.
A friend is like a sister that you never had.
A friend so close they sense it when you're sad.
Friendship is like a wonderful hymn.
You enjoy it until the very end.

I Am a Mother

I am a mother that nurtures her child as if "I were a gardener"
Soiling the foundation set to raise my children.
My child the seed placed down firmly, so that they may grow strong and healthy.
I water them with plenty of love to show them how much I care
As they grow, I feed and talk to them making sure they have a sense of direction.
So that they may grow strong and full of encouragement.
Continuously do I spray them with my words of confidence
Allowing their petals to unfold.
As my children bloom and open up
They learn how to survive looking toward the sun.
Looking for their special nutrients which God provides.
As a mother I tend to them daily, making sure they are not easily uprooted.
Misplaced by the winds of the storms that life may serve.
Therefore, I wrap my arms around them, Keeping them protected.
As I planted them deeply into the soil to assure my job as a mother.
A mother taking care of her garden of children.
She will know I have a well-rounded bunch of flowering children.
Yes, I am a mother.

Silent Screams

My heart aches with pain
While my head hangs in shame.
All alone with notes of songs
Songs that have me feeling alone.
A touch of a hand to soothe my soul
A soul so empty it begins to corrode.
Cry, cry, my weeping heart
My God, I'm tired, I am so tart.
Tart like a lemon, squeezed in the sun
I'm begging, Lord, help me
I'm tired from the run.
No sign of relief
I'm trapped in too deep.
Screaming for justice, set me free
For God is watching and he sees.
The weary mourn with swollen eyes
Tears so heavy, poor child, no pride.
Humble beneath I try to glide
Go with life's flow, I dare to sign.
Thank you God, when You removed the tide.
It made me strong from the strenuous toll
From crawling down that long black road.

Incarceration

I'm incarcerated, I feel like a fly
Caught in the web of a deadly spider.
My heart races at the flutters of my future.
I cannot move but I wiggle around like a dial on a scale awaiting my final measurement.
My life is at the mercy of a spider that paces the web slowly.
It binds me in a waded sack, it prepares itself for attack.
There's nothing that I can do but wish that you will shoo.
I know I ended up in your trap
If only I could turn back.
I hear what sounds like rattling chains
Because I'm slipping away from the poison in may veins.
It's like a cell door never to be reopened.
My eyes are heavy like a steel bed in a cell.
The pain's so painful it feels like hell.
It's dark, the lights have been dimmed.
Will I ever get out, my chances are slim.
I've been eaten alive, no chance to survive.
No one knew that I was here
It was quick, fast, how I disappeared.

Locked Up

Tired is more like it
This routine is making me sick.
Washing my t-shirts and drawers in a sink
There's a smell in my room, it stinks.
I've got these bugs sitting in my basin
One flew in my eyes while washing my face.
How my back aches when my butt's not sore
They gave me a bunk mattress hard as a board.
I get fresh uniforms twice a week
That's not as bad as my dingy, stained sheets.
Who wants to eat wet, wilted lettuce?
The food around here is like a bad habit.
Four to five hours I'm free from the cell
They keep me locked up, can't you tell.
In this jail ain't much to do
If I stay too long, I'm gonna end up cuckoo.
It didn't take long to check me in
The problem is getting out of this state's den.
The guards talk down to me with disrespect
Writing fraudulent reports I didn't expect.
There ain't no justice with the justice system
God be with you if you're here and a Christian.
Darn, it's a challenge trying to do right
When you're around folk that like to fight.
Yeah, I got plenty of stories to tell
I'll tell them all when I'm released from jail.

A Simple Crush

My heart cries out to you
Fluttering swiftly, lightly butterfly wings
Excitement spreading, though fragrant in
A wild garden of purple violets
Sending a peculiar charm of love to my fibers that relish me.

Just One Night

All I need is just one night
Laying in your arms holding me tight.
Soft sweet music to set the mood
Our minds irenic, totally subdued.
Candles burning, setting the stage
I offer my body as your personal slave.
All I need is just one night
A night of romance full of delight.

Drink of the Flesh

Embodied in your flesh, becoming as one
A driving force that makes me crave the juices of your wine.
Be taken oh so gently by the pleasantness of your touch.
Your fervent kisses that make me groan
Sending electricity to places unknown.
Truly addicted to the fruit of the oak.
Alight my body from the deep penetration of your warm, sweaty flesh.
Amorous, my mind incoherent
Indelible in my heart.
Speaking sweet, soft words, sounding lascivious to my ears.
Like a vessel for washing
Cleansing my palates
Refreshing me from the outside in.
Holding me in your arms feels like fine linen.
Your breath on my skin strips me like the needy.
Even though your passion is lethal, I drink more.
How I cherish the exotic bittersweet taste of you.
Consider me a connoisseur of your blended spices
I'm trapped in your memories forever.

Sweet Passion

Ever so slow your lips moving, possessing my thoughts.
Making it hard to sleep, laying so close to you, bestirred.
Your hands melting me like butter in a hot skillet.
Aroused up by the sound of your voice.
Knowing the spiritual side of me is watchful
Grasping on to unite as a pair.
Bright, quivering light from your eyes, sending sparks up my spine.
Never sadden or weary when we are together, never tired.
Time made me seek you out as refuge.
Filled with your sweet pulp, wanting to be safe in your arms.
You give me what I need.
The smell of your skin scented like ladies' slippers.
Flawless without a blemish.
Illustrious silk to my touch, heightening my complete awareness of your existence.
My love for you so finely tuned.
Not ever wanting to disconnect.
My pulse racing, knowing our bodies will collide, joining harmoniously.
Tamarind, filled with your sweet juices.
Flowing together from your smooth, uttered, sweet words.
Not tepid, yet hot like an inferno for your love.
How delectable will it be, that final moment.

Black Coffee on the Sultry Side

What a great book, Milk and Coffee
Still I like my men dark as toffee.
Natural curly hair that looks so hip
A pair of juicy lips so big and thick.
Want my man with a wide-set nose
It's hot, it's sexy, he looks so bold.
Greasy pillowcases, a little dry skin, you see
That's how I like my man, equal to me.
Calluses on his hands prove daddy ain't rich
This means he works for his own, he ain't no bitch.
Ain't nothing wrong with a little mandingo
His voice so deep that it makes me tingle.
Milk in my coffee is not in the plan
I'll take my coffee black like my man.

Broken Trust

He was she, he was her,
I won't be second, I gotta be first.
Jealous when I saw you in the lovers' hold
Ablaze, resentful, losing control.
Refusing to continue to look over my shoulder
I've come to grips this relationship is over.
Speechless about your suave performance
Skillfully done, he even vouched for you.
Blinded by my love for you, I knew
Secretly dividing your time, you shrew.
My mind so disturbed, breaking out into laughter
In accordance with the facts, no happy ever after.
What ever happened to affiance?
Trusting you was my downfall.
Twiddling with my emotions
Did you ever love me at all?
Boy, did you have me fooled
Being compliant, playing by the rules.
Believe me, it's over, I'm done with this mess
You and yo man, I wish you the best.

Love Emotions

Being in love can hit you so fast
It can create an effect that won't pass.
Your thoughts are stranded on the one you love
The constant reminders of the way you snugged.
His soft, strong, masculine hands
That wonder your body like a snake in sand.
Wet, luscious kisses that taste of wine
The sweet taste of his skin like green grapes from the vine.
Your lover's voice reflects the sound of a nice cool breeze
When you hear it, you buckle at the knees.
If he's away, you crave his embrace
His hold is as essential as a virgin in white lace.
Always you feel him when he is yet far
He excites you like a telescope viewing a shooting star.
The way he looks in your eyes makes you purr like a cat
You begin to melt like a tree dripping sap.
His struts as he walks, turns you on like porn
Envisioning his nakedness, you feel reborn.
Being in love can take you on a ride
The only thing left is to take it in stride.
If you recognized these symptoms called love emotions
Just think of it as a hypnotic love potion.

Take Me Away

Please take me away to your secret castle
Take me away, I'm in total rapture.
Wanting you for my own prince charming
Don't let me go, keep me wrapped up in your arms.
In your arms wanting to be lost forever
One life-time of loves endeavor.
Take me away, take me away
To your love castle, where I will stay.
No more Casanova's, you're the one I will love til life's over.
Your my prince indeed on your noble steed.
Riding to our secret land
You and I are holding hands.
Listen to my heart as it pounds
Rest your head on my chest, this is how love sounds.
Ardor, ardor, I feel so lost
Happiness and pleasure will be the only cost.
Please take me away, take me away
To your secret place, I can hardly wait.
Take me away, take me away.

Marriage Proposal

I'm madly in love with you, this is what you said
There isn't a day that goes by that I'm not in your head.
Be your soulmate, your lifelong partner
Written in a letter much sweeter than a rose garden.
Marry me and make me whole
You're the one who holds the key to my soul.
My kids are older and visit me less
When I'm with you I feel at rest.
Today you love me, tomorrow you won't
You'll ask me to love you and make a commitment.
The next day we're friends, you got to be kidding
Time again you've fed me this line.
Unfortunately, buddy, you've run out of time.
Madly in love, marry you, *please*
I would not marry you if you got on one knee.

Love

Love feels like an cheerful song
That you wish could go on and on.
Love is like a kid's favorite teddy
It calms, soothes, and makes you steady.
Love spreads like a deep wide ocean
It's like lavishing your body with your favorite lotion.
Love is like watching the flowers bloom
It takes your breath like a new monsoon.
Love feels like a relaxing massage
It's as lovely as wearing a prom corsage.
Love is taking a walk on the beach
The warm sensation of the sun on your feet.
Love is like watching the autumn leaves
Blowing in the wind as they fly from the trees.
Love makes you laugh when you want to cry
Like a melody of a mother singing a lullaby.
Love fills you up like your favorite meal
The enjoyment like a ride on a ferris wheel.
Love cools you like a swim in the lake
As the sun shines down on your happy face.
Love illuminates you and makes you glimmer
Shining bright as the sky's stars that shimmer.

Romance After Dark

One evening after dark we took a stroll in the park.
You gazed into my eyes
A tingling sensation rose up my thighs.
You placed a kiss on my lips
I felt like doing a flip.
Your hand embracing my shoulder
I begin to feel a little bit bolder.
Placing your hand around my waist
I moved closer to you with grace.
Your mouth explored my body's core
I moaned and yearned, begging for more.
In my ear you hummed my favorite song
As you swayed to the beat I moved along.
We walked holding hands, you were an expert at romance.
I wish that we would never part
A keepsake to remember after dark.

You Were the One

You were the one
I sensed it on our first date.
You were the one
We'd talk until it got late.
You were the one
To be my wife and have my babies.
Well, well, well, umph, well, well,
Wasn't no question about compatibility
Lady, you sealed it with total validity.
I've spooned ya, lady, swooned ya, lady.
You can have all of my money
I know this sounds a little bit funny.
Because you the one that I need
Will you marry me, please?
I ain't never got down like this before
Baby, you make a man beg for more.
My love for you is more than I can explain
That's why I'm asking you today to take my name.
So let me do it right, marry me tonight.
I'll love you till the day we're old
I can't help it but to be bold.
I sensed it on our very first date
Needing to tell you, before it's to late.
Never thought I would fall in love
It was God's doing from heaven above.

Soul Mating

Everyone wanted a love like ours
We were destined for lovers that very first hour.
Soulmates from the very start
I thought that we shared the same heart.
From the moment we met, time stood still
I can never forget that morning on that hill.
Your eyes were shining like the stars in the sky
When I looked at you, I began to feel shy.
I couldn't believe it was love at first sight
You were everything I wanted, including polite.
When I turned around to match your greeting
I could hear, you could hear, each other's hearts beating.
We stood talking about an hour
It was as if we gained special powers.
Finishing each other's sentences was certainly a clue
That you and I were a mate like an old pair of shoes.
When you touched my hand, chills moved up my spine
You felt it too, our bodies intertwine.
You were made for me and I for you
The strange thing was you knew it too.
Soulmates like two love birds
We had fallen in love with just two words.

Tis So Sweet

Life went on for a year, only I did not know
I was drowned in my tears.
Everything I knew began to fade, becoming motionless
Yet on the outside they continued to live.
Tis so sweet to be free
Oh, so many stern voices directing my life choices.
Needing just one touch of a flower
In here I don't have a view to see the spring showers.
Tis so sweet to be free
The sounds I hear are from roaring vents
A smell in the air ,dry, dusty scent.
Hollow, hollow, a feeling of emptiness
Filling a funnel that holds no souls.
Sunshine all over my skin, no not while I'm locked up within.
Tis so sweet to be free
Thoughts of holding my kids in my arms
Sinks me down with sadness as a sinking ship.
Loved living life to the fullest, now I'm being cheated
Open the door and let me walk out.
I don't want to forget what this world is about
Time is still passing, I'm stuck in here.
Release me from my fears with flooding tears
Tis so sweet to be free.

Chocolate Child

Ooh that sun against yo skin
Oh, how it begins to tighten
It darkens, never lightens.
Dry, lacking moisture, they laugh
They ask, on yo skin what's that?
I'm just ashy, you see, when my skin is dry this happens to me.
Look at what the water has done
Yo hair is shrinking, ha ha, like a sponge.
Its just nappy from the pouring rain
After it's pressed it'll get straight again.
Ooh, child, why yo teeth so white
Is it cause yo skin ain't light?
Hearing these things was like taking a smack
Taunting me cause my skin is black.
One boy said your nose is wide
I stood, head up full of pride.
Boy, boy, and you're so ugly
I'm not talking 'bout your looks.
Pointing at his chest, your heart is ugly.
Then I strolled away, carrying my books.

Time Dissipates

Need not persuade me to stay, my love
Kismet, I cannot change what is destined.
No longer do I hold against you a grudge
For it was only time that lost its essence.
Always dinner for two by candlelight
Deep, rich conversation that stimulated us.
As time passed, dinner alone separated by fights
Excuse after excuse leaving in a rush.
Sitting together in our favorite sitting room
Only silence, occasional glances that become stares.
Intentional, intimate brushes as we walk past
Things change, keeping apart, no sparks or flares.
Laying awake at night, hoping you will come home
Daylight sparks through the curtains, still not here.
I was desperate, missing you, waiting by the phone
I'm prepared to move on, conquering my fears.
A house that is sad, bitter anger hides the past
What was good was a distant memory.
I need to be happy, finally content at last.
Farewell, my love, for all left is a remnant.

You Bring Me Peace

Peace is not here in this confusing world
Yet I found comfort in two little girls.
Both beautiful and bright, beaming nothing but sunlight
One with locks of curls is such a delight.
The other with eyes displaying perfect innocence
With a warm pat of her hand beams serenity.
Their joy and laughter consume the day
Making flowers seem boring in the middle of May.
Having delicate hugs like rose petals
Release my tension, I became settled.
Dancing and singing, the world their own
Unhappy, smoothed away by positive energy, succumbed.
Quietness, mind drifting with excitement
Able to pause, relishing when I was
Thanking God for the day I had thee.

No Longer at Liberty

I am at a standstill, everything around me has ceased.
Merriment with smiles, happiness, and frills
So distant, rarely heard, infeasible.
Birds once heard, crickets chirp at day's end
Light brightens the sky from above.
Grass aromatic displaying the scent within
Nature silenced, stale odors, now dull.
Voices, horns sounding from cars
Lost replaced with cries of pain.
Trapped in bondage, mourning from the scars
Feeling empty, hollow, hard to remain sane.
Loved awakening at dawn's day
Exasperated, rising to restricted routine.
Frazzled from pressure, far from calm
Seeking to break free of this terrible brute.
How long before my restrictions' death?
My total existence into disarray
At the end disgraced, searching for dismay.

Storm in Spring

The sun hiding behind the clouds
Grey skies dark and angry.
Rain pouring from the darkness
Searing, running water streams.
Strong loud whistles gusty strong
Humming like a boiling tea kettle.
Leaves stroking from the bouldering trees
Twirling as if, painting an abstract.
Trash cans falling while brushing against the pavement.
Fences rocking back and forth, we can hear the creaking, rocking chair.
A stray cat shivers, then runs for cover.
Barking dogs raveled by the sounds of the wind.
Loud noises thumping, simulating the sound of drums.
Streetlights flickering as tired weak light bulbs.
A storm creates ravage before sunlight.
Silence sneaking into the night, no hail.
Within hours the evening stands silent.
The morning sunlight reawakening nature's dale.

A Child's Room

I am looking into the window of a room that once had life,
That now has no light. It's gloomy, no longer bright.
A room that brought on a smile, unhappy sadden like a cracked road for miles.
As an abandoned house, quiet as a mouse.
Each shadow on the wall reflects the mood of it all.
Once there was laughter heard from the walls.
There's an open book on the windowsill
I strain my eyes to see what it reveals.
It is a childrens book of rhymes now lost forever in time.
The child grew up and moved away, the pages of the book dusty where it lays.

View from a Park Bench

The sun's rays upon my face
My heart beats at an amazing pace.
As I listen silently to the sound of spring
I can hear the sound of fluttering wings.
Distant music that rings sounds of chimes
The chirping of birds takes me back in time.
My mind relaxes to the buzzing of the bees
While watching the birds roam through the trees.
An ardent sensation of feeling whole
A sky so blue my memories shall hold.
Continuous laughter of children's play
Is one of the reasons on the park bench I stayed.
Watching the seesaw go up and down
Not one little child was wearing a frown.
My bare feet brush against the tall green grass
I'm feeling solitude and peace, I wish it could last.
I can smell the aroma of the budding wildflowers
As it begins to rain April showers.
Deep inhalations of the moist cool air
Reminds me of the sweetness of a fresh golden pear.
What an irresistible view from a park bench
Just enjoying nature's pleasures and its scent.

Visualized Portrait

Imagine you're strolling through a park
At a distance you can see the figure of a woman.
A woman that stands so statuesque
She's standing in front of the park pavilion's fountain.
The fountain was most sensual with the carvings of naked cherubs.
You can hear the sounds of yearning from the fountains riverbed.
A cool, misty breeze of sprinkling water across your face.
Her face could not be seen for her back was facing you.
She stood about five-foot ten with slender legs.
The dress she wore accentuated her small waist and curvy hips.
Her arms were narrow as they swung about with long sleek hands swaying with grace.
Closing in at arm's length you notice her hair
Her hair was sandy brown and beautiful as fur.
As she sensed your presence when she turned her head
She had the skin tone of caramel and a hint of red.
Her eyes were as bright as a deer in headlights
Big and brown as they twinkled in the sunlight.
Her brows were thin and neatly shaped, with long eyelashes complimenting her face.
A nose that was perfect and right for her.
Heart-shaped lips not overly stated with a neckline long and slender.
Her breasts are small and perky like plump peaches.
Her smile could light up a room with teeth whiter than pearls.

Here's the Tea

The fountain was surrounded by red roses.
So intrigued by her beauty you close your eyes to savor the moment.
When you open your eyes, much to your surprise
Your woman of grace has vanished from this place.
Looking around she was nowhere to be found.
Was it just a vision you created in your mind?
Perhaps, but you'll never forget the portrait of a woman so fine.

Reflections of a Man

As I lay in a dark-filled room thinking about the sadness and gloom
Once loved by a man, maybe you can't understand.
Once all alone, then his love came along
It was a love that lingered on, the reaction to his touch was all so much.
A man whose words were so deep
I knew he was the one I wanted to keep.
His eyes were like rubies, they hypnotized me truly.
Our hearts danced to the rhythm of the beat
As our bodies indulged underneath the sheets.
Heat, fire, he drives my desire
The sexual pleasure sets my soul on fire.
When he whispers erotica in my ears, the warmness of his breath soothes my fears.
Ooh ah, he makes me quiver as he kisses my softness, he knew how to deliver.
He stole my soul like a thief in the night
I was lost in his love like a plane taking flight.
He sent chills through my soul, like an ice sculpture taking mold.
Leaving emotions oh so deep
His passion made me reach my highest peak.
You can never understand if you lack the pleasure of a man.
A man that weakens you at the knees, because you can't hardly breathe.
To have loved a man many afternoons, hurting inside because he died too soon.

Satan's Introduction

Allow me to introduce myself:
I am the one who sniggers behind your back
I rile you when your enemy attacks
I am remnant and putrefied
I enjoy telling you lies
I nibble at you until you are maimed
I blind you until you are lame
I made you indolent
I laugh because you are indigent
I'm the one that put you in a ghoul
I encourage you to demean others
I secretly do it undercover
I am not chaste
I treat you like garbage waste
I was never affable
I only seek to be afflicting
I want you to know that I don't give advice
I will make you brittle
I'll make you sin until you wither
I am a genie of magic
I will lick you until you're jade
I'll watch you as your life fades
I enjoy scoffing at you
I shun and scuttle you and you can't see me
I am the soothsayer if you follow me

I am a tempter

I want you to incinerate

I do not magnify

I want to break you down

I will drain your happiness

I want to keep your mind off God

Allow me the opportunity to get to know ya

My goal is to kill ya

Most people know me as God's rival

He even introduced me in a book called the Bible

Just like a pimp, I'm full of game

Since I own you, please call me by name

Hello, I'm Lucifer, Satan, the Genie, or the one thrown from above.

Lord, Lord

Lord, Lord, please send me a wife
I promise to love her day and night.
Lord, Lord, I ain't got no mate
I can't remember the last time I had a date.
Lord, Lord, I feel so alone
If You send me a woman, I'll provide her a home.
Lord, Lord, won't You give me some kids
This house is so lonely and extremely big.
Lord, Lord, I want me a family
I'll get the kids a dog or a small pet animal.
Lord, Lord, Lord, she ain't got to be pretty
Instead, I'll settle for a girl that's smart and witty.
Lord, Lord, I'm getting too old
I'm asking You, Lord, for somebody to hold.
Lord, Lord, I looked around the stores
The women looked so mean I ran for the door.
Lord, Lord, I even looked in church
The women in there were even worse.
Lord, Lord, please tell me what to do
I've started getting bald and I'm running out of clues.
Lord, Lord, I don't care if she's old
I'll be patient and kind and treat her like gold.
Lord, Lord, just send me a wife
I don't care if she's Black, Asian, or White.

A Time to Heal

A loved one dies, your heart feels pain
The terrible loss, feeling stressed and strained.
Knowing they're gone, not coming back
Angry with God for not giving you slack.
You prayed to God, pleading for more time
As the clock ticked and began to chime.
Time was up and your loved one had died
Looking peaceful as you stood by their bedside.
Your family member is now at rest
Remember that God always knows best.
Grieving and hurting, saying life is not fair
God will never give you more than you can bear.
God is there for you, making you strong
Let Him comfort and shelter you, you can't go wrong.
Time will heal your pain within
It's replaced with sweet memories of that friend or kin.

Prayer

God is the answer and there's no other way
To get control over your situation, kneel down and pray.
You called your best friend and asked what you should do
On the other line the voice tells you, "I don't have a clue."
While sitting idle you tell yourself,
I really do need to get some help.
God is the only One who holds the key
When you open your eyes, you will see.
You went to the doctors and cried, "Why, why, why."
All He could tell you was, "I'll try, try, try."
God is a doctor that can do all things
He can perform a miracle without being on the scene.
Your attorney said He was great at His game
 But instead of freedom you got numbers for a name.
Why didn't you call God for legal advice
You wouldn't be in jail paying the price.
A conversation with God is all you need
He'll give you the answers, I promise you'll be pleased.

Heavenly Art

We're God's most fabulous creation
A work of art done with patience.
God made us in a variety of shades
Resembling a rainbow on a rainy day.
His hands like a pencil drawing lines
Before we knew it, we were all designed.
God built an art gallery for all of His art
So He could enjoy us from the very start.
He even picked out your beautiful frame
Just before He signed His name.

Am I Condemned

In the beginning, God already knew my ending
He saw my direction before my intersections.
God gave me a thing called choice
Choices were my intersections
Choosing to do wrong broke my connections.
Then He gave me the option of prayer
Prayer is the answer to better directions
If I had followed them, my life would be satisfactory.
"Hey," I say, what's wrong with this picture
No matter what I do, it's contradiction.
What about good and bad
We're hand-picked already, ain't that sad?
The Most High knows me well
Will my chosen path be hell?
Though living, moving through the trails
Am I lost, only He can tell.
Hope gives me a destination
Without it, I wander aimlessly.
In despair, feeling like a derelict child.
If I am docile, is it too late?
My God, have You exiled me
Exscinded me from Your plans?
Yes, Lord, have I follied too long
Feeling futile as an outcast, not belonging.
I sit in rue of the path I've traveled
In time I'll know if I have been disbarred.
I will continue to live and hope thus far.

Part-Time Christian

God don't want no part-time Christian
Partying on Friday, Sunday shouting, "That's right, Bishop."
Cussin' all week and drinkin' booze
God's understanding, but He's tired of those back-sliding moves.
Yes, "God have a problem with mini skirts"
So a Christian shouldn't dress like no whore in church.
God saw you reading that catalog at revival
They read scriptures in church, you didn't have your Bible.
Tithes and offering, God asked for ten percent
When the plate was passed around, you didn't put in a cent.
I'm filled with the Holy Ghost, yes, I'm saved.
God knows about your fornication three nights with Dave.
Skipping out of class, not in Sabbath school
God is getting upset about your worldly bull.
God forgives you but you can't forgive others
He says love your enemy like a sister or brother.
Obviously, God is at the bottom of your list
It's been such a long time He heard a prayer from your lips.
Deacon McDonald, God's been watching your eyes
He saw you looking at Mrs. Maybell's thighs.
God don't want no part-time Christians
He's also talking to you, church bishop.

Garden Rescue

You are a remarkable woman, and you are strong.
Life for you has been like a beautiful garden left unattended.
A garden with the most beautiful and delicate flowers.
Today your flowers are dry and wilted from the lack of the watering hose.
Their soil is crying out for moisture.
Your flowers stoop over, lacking support in their limbs
The mums sing no more to the whispers of the wind.
Your daisies sleep restlessly from the stress of the sun.
Your garden awaits the Caretaker who once nurtured your soul.
You ask, "Did He forget where your petals lay?"
Perhaps He left you and strayed away.
I sit and listen to the humming of a song
For you hummed a tune when you came along.
Today I feel so all alone, no humming, no encouragement to grow healthy and strong.
I need you to nurture my soul in all
When I close my eyes, I am weak and bound.
Thank you, Lord, I hear the sound of the gentle sea
My Gardener has finally remembered me.
It seems so long, but He came along
He sprays my face with amazing grace.
The water quenching my roots as I begin to mold
My daffodils start to take hold.

My garden once forgotten, now all blooms from what was rotten.
I'm alive again though it took time
I am blossoming again, God is always on time.
I assumed my Gardener left me behind because I began to wilt and die.
It was my final moment my last petal fell that the Lord in heaven His arms I felt.
You showered me with Your love, now I'm looking to heaven above.
I am rooted deep in the ground, no longer a need to frown.
I am remarkably strong, a beautiful garden in bloom
My gentle light shines on a sunny day in June.

Weed Picker

Suffocated and surrounded by clovers and ragweed without moisture, crumbling long-time bloom.
Swaying in the air while most of me lost.
Cracking with a gentle brush of the palm, deep down lacking one drink.
Again my Gardener has forgotten me.
I am thirsty and my petals are frail.
Laying in the soil so dry and dusty, blowing with the breeze.
Lips too tight to smile as the sun beams upon me
For the air chafes me instead of cooling me.
Recalling the day, He frowned as He walked about
Mmmm, maybe it was the weeds that took sprout.
My Gardener never liked weeds in His dirt
He only enjoyed the loveliness that sprang from the earth.
What a wonderful gardener He is.
Today I call on my Caretaker to pick my weeds.
When I call on Him, He will dampen me indeed.
The old petals and stems will be replaced
Reborn again without my weeds
My Gardener shall plant the perfect seed.
When the sun shines upon me, I will flourish
Hands will touch me, and I will stand firm.
His watering hose making me complete
Smiling bright as my flowers blossom.

Weeds uninvited to live among my bulbs
Only sweet things in my garden to love.
I've called upon my Gardener, He is here to revive me
He's even planted peace lilies.
Therefore, I love my Gardener
Why do I doubt Him, maybe a little silly.

At Rest

Each of our lives set as a clock
God planned the time that it would stop.
It's a time we all shall fall asleep
Our burdens now underneath our feet.
Awaiting the moment of His return
An exciting moment we always yearned.
Dying isn't really bad at all
You're just resting until your name is called.
To stand before God to claim your prize
What a celebration it will be the day we rise.
So hush, my child, try not to weep
This is our time to be at peace.
Passing away was already on the map
So, rejoice, don't cry, we're just taking a nap.

God's Promise

Lord, You said call when I'm in a jam
No matter what I did, come as I am.
I'm in a terrible place, You see
You said call on You, You'll rescue me.
Satan attacked me when I let down my guard
He dealt me a hand with losing cards.
Why didn't I walk away, put my cards in the stack
And run to the Lord and never look back?
Satan wanted to win, he was winning the game
Then I remembered these words, "Just call out My name."
I remembered You loved the weak, lame and poor
No matter what I did, You still open Your door.
Things got steep, Lord, I was lame and weak, Lord
Played a losing game, Lord, now I feel ashamed, Lord.
You took me as I am, no longer in a jam
You took my hand just as I am.

Love Fizzes

Never been in love, though I had many lovers
Hiding my heart safely, keeping it covered.
Protected from hurt that love brings
No risk, no pain that can transcend.
Doubt into your world of insecurities
Safely guarding your heart with security.
That love won't get you down, down.
Leaving you naked as if your lover had abandoned you
Outside yourself, looking for something new.
Love don't last, its hype fizzes
Relief ends and the fizz is gone.
Interest mellows, yonder sway gone.
Never loved, only loss fills the room.
False emotions flowing eventually brewing
Into nothing, that is love not worth pursuing.

Love

Beautiful, copious love holds no boundaries
Love is the existence of emotions
Requiring nothing and giving all,
All that soars is limitless
Giving without question or fear
Being able to love with friendship that says I am here
Here to hold your hand when everyone else sears.

Unsound Mind

Leather don't break, is what I said
I refused to let the world get in my head.
Worrying about my mind being broken
Foolishly I left my heart open.
Stress can put you in a strange position
When your heart is broken, it's an imposition.
As the world overcrowds your mind
You begin to search for a world that's sound.
If it's your heart at stake
From the lack of love, it breaks.
Feeling overwhelmed can leave you confused
Separate the facts to relieve the blues.
You got to keep a song in your heart
To keep your mind from straying afar.
A broken mind you can't repair
A broken heart will leave you scarred.
Both of these things work together
If one malfunctions, it's not forever.
Unbalanced, unfocused, and a little bit wavy
Leaving you searching for a way out of slavery.
Slavery of uncertainties that weigh you down
Until there's nothing left but hopelessness and frowns.

Teresia Simmons-Ursch

Little Bennie

There was a boy named begging Benny
He was so poor, he didn't have a penny.
Benny was happy, although he was poor
He had good-hearted neighbors to put food on his door.
They gave him brown bread, how wonderful, he said.
He pulled out some chicken, what finger-licking.
There was also corn that was sweet and warm.
Benny had a huge baked potato, he sniffed it like a garden tomato.
He had chocolate on his face from the yummy slice of cake.
They even brought him a pie, it was a mincemeat pie.
Now his belly was full as he sat on his stool.
Benny knew he was blessed as he unbuttoned his vest.
He folded his hands and began to kneel
As he thanked the Lord for his blessed meal.
Benny was a boy who only had one leg
He couldn't get a job, he had to beg instead.
This is a rhyme about a poor little boy
Poor little Benny who had to beg door to door.

The Fat Rat

There once was a rat that was oh so fat.
He had an appointment to sing for a very fine king.
He wore a black suit, oh what a hoot.
The suit was so snug like a bug in a rug.
The rat begins to sway as he heard the music play.
He began to croon to the band too soon.
His voice begins to squeal like a rusty little wheel.
The king laughed at the rat when he dropped his little hat.
He did all that he could, but was just too fat.
The rat took a quick dip, hoping to grab it by the tip.
He tried to wiggle, wiggle down to the floor
So out of breath he couldn't take it no more.
The rat knew he was in a pickle as he rubbed his shiny whiskers.
The rat bowed to the crowd as they laughed out loud.
There was a sound of a rip like a tearing of a slip
His trousers he had torn wide open like a door on a barn.
When he heard the crack, he began to hold his back.
His jacket button popped as he began to hop.
His stomach was so big that it danced a funny jig.
He pounced on his hat as he hopped along, to the melody of an English song.
His hat got stuck on his patterned leather shoe
He kicked it and shook it, but it was stuck like glue.

The frog king laughed until he lost his wig
It flew across the room and hit lady pig.
When the show was over, the king clapped and cheered
It was one of the best performances he had seen in years.
The king patted the chubby little rat on his back
As he smiled at the rat and invited him back.

*Hope you enjoyed the art work in the book.
It's just a few pieces that I thought you would enjoy viewing.
Look out for my next two children's books that I have written
that will be in a bookstore and online for your childs entertainment.
The titles are "The Cat and the Rat" and "The Duck That Cried Shark".
Will post on social media when they are ready to be purchased.*

Thank you to all my supportive readers.

Teresia Simmons-Ursch

www.ingramcontent.com/pod-product-compliance
Lightning Source LLC
LaVergne TN
LVHW011738060526
838200LV00051B/3219